D0912936

JENNETTE McCURDY

Mary Boone

Mitchell Lane
PUBLISHERS

P.O. Box 196
Hockessin, Delaware 19707
Visit us on the web: www.mitchelllane.com
Comments? email us: mitchelllane@mitchelllane.com

Mitchell Lane
PUBLISHERS

Printing   1   2   3   4   5   6   7   8   9

A Robbie Reader
Contemporary Biography

Abigail Breslin	Albert Pujols	Alex Rodriguez
Aly and AJ	Amanda Bynes	AnnaSophia Robb
Ashley Tisdale	Brenda Song	Brittany Murphy
Charles Schulz	Dakota Fanning	Dale Earnhardt Jr.
David Archuleta	Demi Lovato	Donovan McNabb
Drake Bell & Josh Peck	Dr. Seuss	Dwayne "The Rock" Johnson
Dylan & Cole Sprouse	Eli Manning	Emily Osment
Emma Watson	Hilary Duff	Jaden Smith
Jamie Lynn Spears	**Jennette McCurdy**	Jesse McCartney
Jimmie Johnson	Johnny Gruelle	Jonas Brothers
Jordin Sparks	Justin Bieber	Keke Palmer
Larry Fitzgerald	LeBron James	Mia Hamm
Miley Cyrus	Miranda Cosgrove	Raven-Symoné
Selena Gomez	Shaquille O'Neal	Story of Harley-Davidson
Syd Hoff	Taylor Lautner	Tiki Barber
Tom Brady	Tony Hawk	Victoria Justice

Library of Congress Cataloging-in-Publication Data
Boone, Mary.
 Jennette McCurdy / by Mary Boone.
   p. cm. — (A robbie reader)
 Includes bibliographical references and index.
 ISBN 978-1-58415-900-1 (library bound)
 1. McCurdy, Jennette, 1992- —Juvenile literature. 2. Television actors and actresses—United States—Biography—Juvenile literature. 3. Singers—United States—Biography—Juvenile literature. I. Title.
 PN2287.M54547B66 2010
 791.4502'8092—dc22
 [B]
                                                              2010019387

ABOUT THE AUTHOR: Mary Boone has written 15 books for young readers, including Blue Banner Biographies about David Wright, Corbin Bleu, and Vanessa Anne Hudgens. Mary, her husband, Mitch, and her children, Eve and Eli, live in Tacoma, Washington, where they regularly watch *iCarly*.

TABLE OF CONTENTS

Words in **bold** type can be found in the glossary.

Jennette McCurdy is all smiles as she arrives at the 2009 Prism Awards in Beverly Hills. While she loves acting, she hopes to go to film school and someday write and direct her own movies.

Big Dreams
for a Tiny Girl

Jennette McCurdy was just six years old when she boldly announced her career plans.

She and her family had just seen *Star Wars Episode 1: The Phantom Menace* at a California theater. Before the movie even ended, the tiny girl turned to her mother and said, "Mommy, I want to act."

Much like parents whose kindergartners or first graders declare they're going to grow up to be cowboys or astronauts, Jennette's parents, Mark and Debbie McCurdy, said something along the lines of: "That's nice, honey."

There was no way the McCurdys could have imagined that their shy little girl would someday have the talent and spirit to make it in show business. But she would. By the time she was a young adult, Jennette had become one of the hottest television actresses around. She was also kicking off a promising musical career.

Jennette was born June 26, 1992. When she was three years old, her mother was **diagnosed** (dy-ug-NOHST) with breast cancer. Her mother required months of treatment for the disease. It often left her too tired to spend much time with her daughter.

In order to distract their little sister, Jennette's older brothers—Dustin, Scott, and Marcus—would watch movies with her. *Star Wars* was a favorite. The siblings watched it over and over again.

"I loved the line, 'May the force be with you,'" Jennette told the *Orange County Register.* The saying made her feel powerful at a very scary time in her life.

When Debbie McCurdy finished her treatment, the family celebrated by going to see the newest *Star Wars* movie. After watching the action on the big screen, Jennette knew she wanted to become an actress.

"I hounded [my parents] for about a year," she told *The Orange County Register.* " 'Did you get me an agent? Did you?' "

Finally, Debbie found out how she could help Jennette achieve her dream. She had a photographer take **headshots** (HED-shots) of her, and she found an agent. Before long, Jennette was at her first **audition** (aw-DIH-shun).

Jennette took a lot of small jobs before she acted in a movie. She had a minor role in the 2004 thriller *Breaking Dawn*.

Landing Her First Big Roles

As much as she wanted to be a star, Jennette did not head straight to Hollywood. Instead, she started by auditioning for parts in **commercials** (kuh-MER-shuls) and in plays for local theaters. It was a good way to ease into show business.

"For the first year, I was so nervous," she told *The Orange County Register*. "I'd have butterflies in my stomach. I'd go to the bathroom about 10 times. I was probably more nervous than any kid could get."

Before long, she landed her first jobs: a television commercial for a dentist, and playing

Debbie McCurdy, left, has been supportive of her daughter's career. She and Jennette attended the 2009 Revlon Run/Walk for Women in Los Angeles. The event raised money to help battle cancer in women. The cause is dear to the McCurdy family.

Jennette walked the red carpet for the first time when *Breaking Dawn* **premiered** (preh-MEERD). She was just twelve years old at the time.

actress Kathie Lee Gifford's daughter Cassidy in a *MadTV* skit.

Soon, she got a new agent who found her even more jobs. She made a national commercial for Domino's Pizza, and then, in 2002, she got a small part on the TV show *CSI*.

11

As she gained experience (ek-SPEER-ee-unts), Jennette began to audition for bigger roles on better-known shows. She got parts on *Strong Medicine, Medium,* and *Judging Amy.* She played kids in trouble in all three shows.

To help her play these parts, Jennette remembered how she felt when her mother was ill. But she wasn't sad and serious all the time. In fact, she got parts on **comedies** (KAH-meh-deez). She appeared on *Malcolm in the Middle, Will and Grace,* and *Zoey 101.*

While she was playing the part of a tough, cool kid on *Zoey 101,* she caught the attention of Dan Schneider, the show's creator. Schneider had also created *Drake and Josh,* and he'd been

In 2006, Jennette got a small part in *Will and Grace*. In the episode, the cast went to a *Sound of Music* sing-along. Jennette acted alongside Debra Messing, Megan Mullally, and Sean Hayes.

thinking about a new series. The idea was still in the planning stages, but he sensed Jennette might be right for one of the parts. He was right.

Dan Schneider chose a winning cast for *iCarly*. He gives Jerry Trainor a lift as Jennette, Miranda Cosgrove, and Nathan Kress laugh along.

CHAPTER THREE

Getting Wacky with *iCarly*

Dan Schneider wanted to make a funny show with strong characters. He did that when he created *iCarly*. The show is about a girl named Carly (played by Miranda Cosgrove) who produces a web show with her friends Sam (Jennette) and Freddie (Nathan Kress). Actor Jerry Trainor plays Spencer, Carly's brother and legal **guardian** (GAR-dee-un).

During the show-within-a-show **webcasts** (WEB-kasts), the young actors tape funny segments and skits. They dance. They make soup in a toilet. And they play crazy games, like "Hey, What Am I Licking?"

15

It is that kind of wackiness that has made *iCarly* a huge hit. The show first aired on the Nickelodeon network in September 2007. Two and a half years later, more than 11 million people were still tuning in each time *iCarly* was on TV. The show was named Favorite TV Show at the 2009 and 2010 Nickelodeon Kids' Choice Awards. It had also been **nominated** (NAH-mih-nay-ted) for the award in 2008.

Jennette's character, Sam Puckett, is selfish and impolite. It is a far cry from her off-screen personality. Schneider told the *Orange County Register,* "Sam is rude . . . and a little bit mean. And then you yell 'Cut!' and Jennette is the sweet little girl who couldn't be nicer. It's pretty cool to see."

Jennette told *Crushable.com* that, while she's kinder than Sam, she does like to joke around. "I think I'm kind of wacky and crazy. I just don't like pushing people down and slamming them into lockers and eating bacon all the time," she said. "I think I have a great character that I get to do a lot with. She allows for a lot of fun experiences."

Jennette sparkled next to Miranda Cosgrove at the 2009 Teen Choice Awards. Jennette's sequin dress put her on many critics' "best dressed" lists.

What kind of fun experiences?

"I don't know who else besides us could say they've run over a microwave filled with toothpaste in a monster truck," she told the *Los Angeles Times*.

Point taken.

Jennette is not only an actress. She is also a country music singer.
She combined those two talents when she performed in Faith Hill's
music video for "The Way You Love Me."

Music and Movies

Jennette and fellow *iCarly* actor Jerry Trainor acted together again in a TV movie called *Best Player.* Trainor plays Quincy, a 32-year-old video-game champion who lives in his parents' basement. He enters a **tournament** (TOR-nuh-munt) to win some much-needed prize money. His chances look good until he meets Jennette's character, Prodigy. She could be good enough to beat him. The movie was filmed in Canada in early 2010.

Jennette filmed another made-for-TV movie as well. *Fred: The Movie* is based on a popular Internet character created by Lucas Cruikshank. In the movie, Jennette portrays Fred's friend, Bertha.

After she made her mark as an actress, Jennette set her sights on becoming a big-time recording artist. "I've been working on it more recently, but I've actually always kind of had a passion for music and I've had a lot of **inspiration** [in-spuh-RAY-shun] from music," she told *Crushable.com*.

Her first single, "So Close," was released in March 2009. Two months later, she released a second single, "Homeless Heart." She wrote that song in honor of Cody Waters, a friend who died of cancer.

Critics and fans alike hailed her strong, bluesy voice. Jennette announced that her first album would be released on June 30, 2009, but that date came and went with no album. Then, in July 2009, she announced she had signed a deal with Capitol Records Nashville.

In March 2010, Jennette reported on her official website that she'd finally finished work on the album. It would be called *The Story of My Life*. A month later, samples of six songs from it were released to allow fans to vote for

Jennette celebrated the 2009 Country Music Awards with country music hotshots (back row, left to right): Jimi Westbrook, Keith Urban, Phillip Sweet, Capitol Records Nashville President Mike Dungan, Darius Rucker, Kimberly Roads; (front row, left to right): Karen Fairchild, Walker Hayes, and Luke Bryan.

her first radio single. "Not That Far Away" won. When fans heard it, they were thrilled. They could hardly wait for the album to be released.

Jennette hangs out with B.O.B. at the 2009 premiere of *Monsters vs. Aliens.* One of her idols, Reese Witherspoon, is the voice for the lead character, Susan Murphy/Ginormica (jy-NOR-mih-kuh).

Goals and Giving Back

Starring in a hit TV show, winning awards, and recording a solo album are goals some people spend their entire careers trying to achieve. Jennette McCurdy has done all of that—but she wants to do more.

The young performer dreams of a career both in front of and behind the camera. She wants to move from television to the big screen.

"I would absolutely love to go into directing," she told *TheStarScoop.com*.

Like most folks, she has her favorite entertainers. She has long been a fan of Harrison Ford (whose breakout role was in *Star Wars*) and was **starstruck** when Reese

Witherspoon told her that she watches *iCarly* with her daughter. Still, if she could choose any actors with whom she could work, she's happy to dream big.

"I would love to work with Johnny Depp," she told *Scholastic News*. "I think he's the coolest. He's awesome. And Meryl Streep is absolutely amazing. Doing a movie with her would be the best."

Jennette loves her fans. She often sends them updates about her career through videos on her YouTube channel.

While Jennette's musical career is taking off, she doesn't plan to give up her television and movie work. "I have a strong, strong passion for acting, so I don't ever think I could leave it!" she told *Portrait* magazine.

Is a role opposite Depp or Streep in her future? That remains to be seen. For now, Jennette is grateful for the opportunities she's been given. She also enjoys support from her "frans"—a term she uses for her fans/friends.

As busy as she is, Jennette still finds time to give back. In 2010, she was named a StarPower **Ambassador** (am-BAH-sah-dor) for the Starlight Children's Foundation. Nathan Kress also volunteers with this organization. It works to make the lives of ill children better by bringing them entertainment and by helping them learn in school.

Using her personal "star power" to brighten the lives of young patients through hospital visits or online chats is like icing on the cake for Jennette. She's not only doing what she's always wanted to do, but she is also able to help others. She would like to see other young people give their time and energy to bring cheer to people who need it the most.

Jennette hangs out with fan Brittney Hamilton at the 2008 Starlight Children's Foundation "Sparkling Sundae" event in Los Angeles. Jennette also volunteers for other organizations, including St. Jude Children's Research Hospital, Safe Kids USA, and Invisible Children, Inc.

"Here she is, living her dream," Debbie McCurdy told the *Orange County Register*. "It's really, really quite incredible."

CHRONOLOGY

1992 Jennette Michelle Faye McCurdy is born June 26 in Los Angeles to Mark and Debbie McCurdy.

1995 Jennette finds out that her mother has breast cancer.

2000 She lands her first role on *MadTV*.

2002 She has a role on *CSI: Crime Scene Investigation*.

2005 Jennette is nominated for a Young Artist Award for Best Performance in a Television Series/Guest Starring Young Actress for her performance in *Strong Medicine*.

2007 She lands a starring role in the Nickelodeon TV series *iCarly*.

2008 She is nominated for a Young Artist Award for *iCarly* and for her role as Dory Sorenson in the made-for-TV movie *The Last Day of Summer*.

2009 With her sights on becoming a country music singer, she releases her first single, "So Close," on March 9. Later that year, she signs an album deal with Capitol Records Nashville. She is nominated for a Teen Choice Award in the "Best Sidekick" category.

2010 She films the Nickelodeon made-for-TV movie *Best Player* with Jerry Trainor. *Fred: The Movie* premieres on Nickelodeon; McCurdy plays the role of Fred's pal Bertha. Her album *The Story of My Life* is set for release.

SELECTED FILMOGRAPHY

2010	*Fred: The Movie* (TV movie)
	True Jackson, VP (TV, guest role)
2009	*iDate a Bad Boy* (TV movie)
	iFight Shelby Marx (TV movie)
	iQuit iCarly (TV movie)
2008	*True Jackson, VP* (TV, guest role)
	iCarly: iGo to Japan (TV movie)
2007–present	*iCarly* (TV series)
2007	*The Last Day of Summer* (TV movie)
	Lincoln Heights (TV, guest role)
2006	*Will and Grace* (TV, guest role)
	Close to Home (TV, guest role)
2005	*Zoey 101* (TV, guest role)
	Law and Order: Special Victims Unit (TV, guest role)
	Judging Amy (TV, guest role)
	Malcolm in the Middle (TV, guest role)
2004	*Breaking Dawn*
	Strong Medicine (TV, guest role)
2003	*Malcolm in the Middle* (TV, guest role)
2002	*CSI: Crime Scene Investigation* (TV, guest role)
2000	*MadTV* (TV, guest role)

DISCOGRAPHY

Album
2010 *The Story of My Life*
Singles
2010 "Not That Far Away"
2009 "So Close"
     "Homeless Heart"

FIND OUT MORE

For Young Readers

Corse, Nicole. *iCarly Scrapbook*. New York: Scholastic Inc, 2009.

Leavitt, Amie Jane. *Miranda Cosgrove*. Hockessin, Delaware: Mitchell Lane Publishers, 2009.

Morreale, Marie. "A Talk with Jennette McCurdy." *Scholastic News*, October 19, 2007. http://www2.scholastic.com/browse/article.jsp?id=3748275

Works Consulted

Eleni. "Jennette McCurdy Interview." *Portrait*, March 2009. http://www.portraitmagazine.net/interviews/jennettemccurdy2.html

"Exclusive Q&A with *iCarly*'s Jennette McCurdy." *J-14*, n.d. http://www.j-14.com/2009/12/exclusive-q-a-with-icarlys-jen

Hale, Mike. "Carly and Friends Face Real Adolescent Angst." *The New York Times*, December 5, 2009. http://tv.nytimes.com/2009/12/05/arts/television/05carly.html?_r=1

Hatch, Danielle. "sheSam on *iCarly*." (Peoria) *Journal Star*, November 19, 2008. http://www.pjstar.com/entertainment/x2067099627/sheSam-on-iCarly

"Jennette McCurdy." *The Star Scoop.com*, 2007. http://www.thestarscoop.com/2007/jennette-mccurdy.php

Katz, Nikki. "Exclusive: Jennette McCurdy Chats Meeting Her Idol." *Crushable.com*, March 27, 2009. http://crushable.com/entertainment/exclusive.jennette-mccurdy-chats-meeting-her-idol/

Larsen, Peter. "The 15-Year-Old TV Sidekick." *The Orange County Register*, September 13, 2009. http://www.ocregister.com/entertainment/icarlyjennettemccurdynickelodeonseries-21632--.html

Martin, Denise. " 'iCarly': Ruler of the Tweens." *Los Angeles Times*, April 28, 2009. http://articles.latimes.com/2009/apr/28/entertainment/et-icarly28

Shen, Maxine. "*iCarly* Pals Get Own Movie." *New York Post*, October 19, 2009. http://www.nypost.com/p/entertainment/tv/item_pSjCy1tdcgZgsVgPciDpzJ

On the Internet

Jennette McCurdy's Official Web Site
http://jennettemccurdy.com

Official Website for *iCarly*
http://www.icarly.com

Starlight Children's Foundation
http://www.starlight.org/

GLOSSARY

ambassador (am-BAH-sah-dor)—A person who speaks and volunteers for an organization.

audition (aw-DIH-shun)—A tryout, generally by an actor, musician, or dancer.

comedy (KAH-muh-dee)—A show that is meant to be funny or silly.

commercials (kuh-MER-shuls)— Advertisements broadcast on radio or television.

diagnose (dy-ug-NOHS)—To recognize a disease by signs and symptoms.

guardian (GAR-dee-un)—Someone who takes care of another person.

headshot (HED-shot)—A photograph of someone's head and face.

inspiration (in-spuh-RAY-shun)—Someone or something that makes you want to do great things.

premiere (preh-MEER)—First showing.

nominated (NAH-mih-nay-ted)—Named as a possibility for receiving an award.

starstruck—Impressed by someone simply because he or she is famous.

tournament (TOR-nuh-munt)—A series of games or contests.

webcast (WEB-kast)—A video or other file shown over the Internet.

INDEX